WordPress Ultimate Guide

A step by step guide in creating your blog in 30 minutes or less

Table of Contents

Introduction ....

Chapter 1: An Overview to WordPress ....

Chapter 2: The WordPress Dashboard ....

Chapter 3: Crafting your Blog Contents ....

Chapter 4: The WordPress Community ....

Conclusion ....

Check Out My Other Books ....

Copyright

Copyright © 2013 NrBooks.net

All rights reserved. No part of this book may be reproduced in any form or by any electronic or mechanical means including information storage and retrieval systems – except in the case of brief quotations in articles or reviews – without the permission in writing from its publisher, NrBooks.net.

All brand names and product names used in this book are trademarks, registered trademarks, or trade names of their respective holders. We are not associated with any product or vendor in this book.

Introduction

I want to thank you and congratulate you for downloading the book, *"WordPress Ultimate Guide: A step by step guide in creating your blog in 30 minutes or less."*

This book contains proven steps and strategies on how to start blogging on WordPress as well as how to expand your community and connection on WordPress. Specifically, this book talks about how to create your posts on WordPress as well as customize your blog. It also discusses how to get connected to other people and how to make your WordPress community grow.

Thanks again for downloading this book, I hope you enjoy it!

Chapter 1: An Overview to WordPress

We are all familiar to blogs. Perhaps most of us—if not all—have already read at least one blog entry in our entire life as Internet users.

Why do we blog?

A blog (which is a combination of the words *web* and *log*) is a site which features different entries called as *entries*. Essentially, when you blog, you post a content online—whether it is a text post, or a photo, or a video, or any multimedia—and then publish it on your blog.

Because blogs are usually for free, many people are being hooked on this activity. More so, blogging serves as the online journal of people, where they regularly write their thoughts, opinions, or ideas and generally express themselves. But more than the personal purposes, blogs can also be used for businesses and some other purposes, which are more formal in terms of the contents and objectives.

Basically, there are six basic reasons as to why people engage to blogging. Some people maintain blogs for personal purposes, while some use it for their businesses. Blogs are also being used by people in the media and journalism industry, as well as by people in the government. Other people also make use of blogging for citizen journalism as well as other professional categories.

   a. *Personal.* There are some people who consider their blogs as their online diary or journal, where they document every single detail of their life. Personal bloggers mainly discuss on their blogs things that are related to their personal lives—such as their family, friends, pets, and interests. Basically, it is like they are opening a window for other people to have an overview of what their life is like.

b. *Business.* While other people blog for personal gain, others blog because they want to earn. They make use of their blogs to promote the company that they are in or endorse their personal businesses. Blog is said to be an effective medium for businesses since it can easily reach people. Moreover, businesspeople make use of blogs because it is convenient and it helps them easily provide information to their possible customers. People can also give their feedback to these businesses, which makes the transaction easier.

c. *Media or journalism.* Even media companies, such as TV networks and news agencies, also make use of blogging in providing information as well as insights on current events. Since blog platforms are easy and fast to use, these agencies can easily give their contents to the people. They can post news stories, photos, videos, podcasts, and other media that can help disseminate important information and stories.

d. *Government.* Media companies are not the only big groups that make use of blogging. Even the government also engages in blogs. Usually, the government's official blogs include text posts, photos, videos, and other contents that are important for the interaction and connection between the government and the citizen. Some government officials also integrate government blogs to their Twitter and Facebook accounts for it to reach a wider range of people.

e. *Citizen journalism.* Media nowadays has already moved from the traditional form to the modern one. Nowadays, official news agencies are not the only ones who can disseminate news stories; even common citizens can. Of course, these citizens do not have their own newspaper lines as well as news websites, so they just make use of blogging in sharing their journalistic stories. They create blog accounts which serve as their official site in providing current events and other relevant stories.

f. *Professional.* There are also professional bloggers who write blog contents for other companies as well as websites. There are some blog networks which hire writers or bloggers who will provide the contents for them. These contents can be about anything that they wish to discuss. Likewise, there are some blogs that advertise products. Of course, the blogger gets paid by the advertisers afterward.

WordPress at a glance

There are a lot of websites out there that are intended for blogging, and most of these options are entirely for free. And one of the most popular blogging sites on the web nowadays is *WordPress*.

WordPress is a site that was first launched way back in 2003 by the Automattic team. It is an open source content management system, which means the developers work for the maintenance and functionality of the site while the users enjoy its services for free. WordPress was created by and for the community of bloggers out there. It was meant for creating, publishing, as well as maintaining blog contents, which can be about anything that the bloggers want to write about.

More than a decade later, the community in WordPress has undeniably grown exponentially. More and more people are being engaged to blogging, thus creating WordPress accounts. Because of this, the team from Automattic has decided to expand the site by creating two versions: WordPress.com and WordPress.org.

WordPress.com

WordPress.com, which was launched in 2005, is said to be the version that is easier to use as compared to the other one. All the data that are being created on WordPress.com are hosted by WordPress, which means WordPress is responsible for storing and managing all the data and information created by the users as well as maintaining all the "behind-the-scenes technology" that are necessary to be able to display the blog contents online.

When you use WordPress.com, all you have to do is just log in to your account, and then write your content and click publish after. You won't even have to do anything else after publishing your blog content; WordPress got your back.

WordPress.com is the hosted version, meaning there is no need for you to download any software and install it. Everything happens quickly and easily.

However, there are still some limitations when you are using this version. It does not allow you install plugins and even custom themes. It will not even let you customize the base code files. This applies most especially if you are using the free version. You can still do some customization on your blog using the CSS feature of WordPress, but it is only available once you upgrade. Of course, you have to pay in order for you to upgrade your WordPress account.

WordPress.org

WordPress.org, on the other hand, offers self-hosted application for users. Unlike WordPress.com, this version requires you to download and install the software which you can download from WordPress' web site (http://wordpress.org). Of course, WordPress.org has a lot of differences from WordPress.com. This version now offers several tools and resources that will take your blogging experience to the next level.

This version gives you the ability to use plugins for your blog, which you will need for enhancing your SEO, managing your blog comments, integrating your account to your other social media accounts, and many more.

This version also allows you to customize your blog's theme. There are lots of free themes on the Free Themes Directory of WordPress that you can choose from and use to enhance the appearance of your blog.

In order for you to use this version, you have to pay for a web host—the company that will provide the space where you can store all the data from your website and blog—whose main task is to store and serve the content of your blog to your visitors. Once you already have a web host, you may opt to register your own domain for your blog—which also requires a fee—and then publish your own blog.

Chapter 2: The WordPress Dashboard

One of the basics of WordPress that you have to understand well is the *dashboard*. Basically, this is where all the magic happens.

Working around the Dashboard

The WordPress dashboard, as shown in Figure 2.1, is considered as the control panel because this is where all the quick links as well as relevant and important areas are located. Everything that you do on your blog is done on the dashboard, so it is important that you know the dashboard very well.

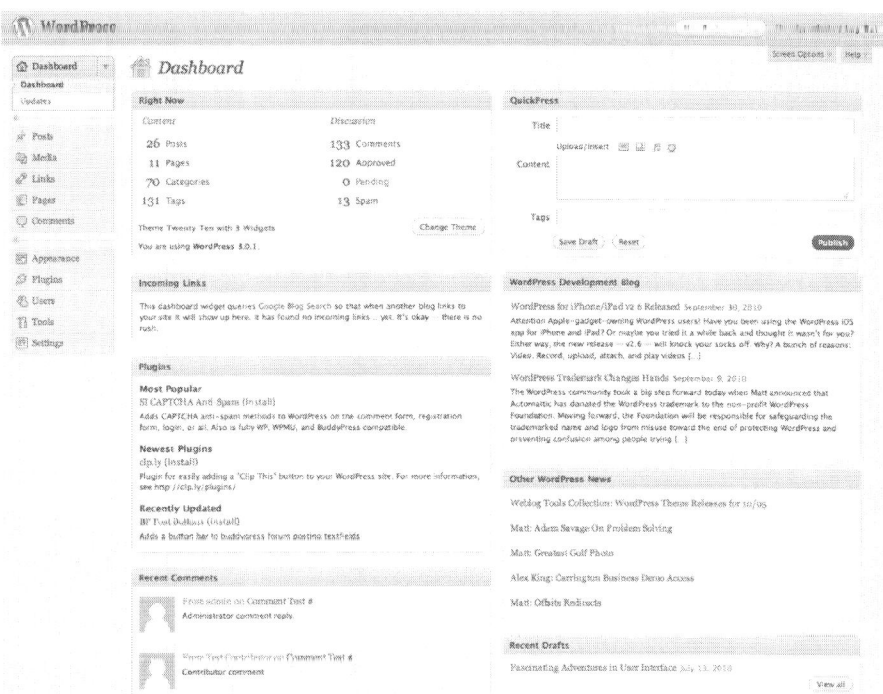

Figure 2.1. The WordPress Dashboard. Photo courtesy: real-estate-website.ca)

As you can see, there are eight modules or sections seen on the WordPress dashboard. These modules include the following: Right Now, Recent Comments, Incoming Links, Plugins, QuickPress, WordPress Development Blog, Other WordPress News, and Recent Drafts.

By default, when you first log in to your WordPress account, all the modules appear extended on the dashboard. However, you can change the order in which these modules appear, which means you can either expand (or open) and collapse (close) the individual modules just by clicking anywhere within the module's title bar. The idea is that you use your dashboard for the modules that you use regularly, so you may opt to close those which you seldom use. You can open those modules anytime you want, anyway, so it will be handy if you close some of them for the meantime.

Right Now

As the name itself suggests, The Right Now module, as shown in Figure 2.2, basically tells you what is happening in your blog *right now*. It gives you an overview as to how many posts you have already created as well as how many pages are there, the number of blog categories that you have, as well as the number of tags and comments. All of this information appears just below the Content and Discussion headers.

a. *The number of the posts.* This shows you the exact number of posts that you have already created. When you click the number, you will be brought to the Edit Posts page where you can edit your posts.

b. *The number of pages.* This shows you the exact number of pages that your blog has. Of course, the number showed here changes whenever you add or delete a page. You can also click this, which will redirect you to the Edit Pages page where you can view and edit your pages.

c. *The number of categories.* This shows you the number of categories that your blog has, which you can always add and delete. You may also click this link and you will be redirected to the Categories page, to view and edit your old and new categories.

d. *The number of tags.* This shows you how many tags are already there in your blog. Of course, this always changes are you add and delete ones. When you click this link, you will be brought to the Tags page where you can add new tags as well as view and edit the old ones.

e. *The number of comments.* This shows you the exact number of comments that people have posted on your blog. There are the approved and pending comments as well as the ones that are marked as spams. When you click these links, you will be taken to the Edit Comments page where you can edit the comments on your blog.

Aside from these, you can also find in the Right Now section which theme you are using for your blog, which when clicked redirects you to the Manage Themes page to view and activate themes on your blog. You can also change your theme on the Manage Themes page. Moreover, you can see there how many widgets you are using on your blog, which also when clicked redirects you to the Widgets page where you can edit, move, or remove the widgets. Lastly, you can also see the WordPress version that you are using on your blog.

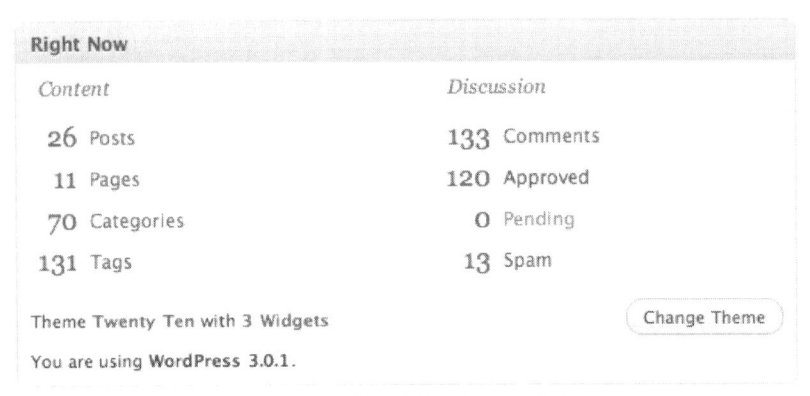

Right Now	
Content	*Discussion*
26 Posts	133 Comments
11 Pages	120 Approved
70 Categories	0 Pending
131 Tags	13 Spam
Theme Twenty Ten with 3 Widgets	Change Theme
You are using **WordPress 3.0.1**.	

Figure 2.2. The Right Now module.

Recent Comments

This module, which includes all the information about the recent comments posted on your blog, is located right below the Right Now module. The things that you will find in this module are the following:

a. *Most recent comments and who wrote them.* This shows you a maximum of five most recent comments published to your WordPress blog. The names of the authors of these comments will also be shown to you, along with their avatars.

b. *Link to the post which the comment was posted.* This shows you the title of the post in which the comment was put on. This link is placed right next to the name of the person who created that comment. When you click the link, you will be redirected to the post in the Admin panel.

c. *Excerpt of the comment.* You will also be shown a short excerpt of the comment left on your blog.

d. *Comment management links.* These are the links that appear whenever you hover your mouse cursor on a comment. There are five links there, which allow you to: (1) "Unapprove" a comment, edit a comment, reply to a comment, mark a comment as spam, and put a comment to trash.

e. *View all button.* Since only five comments are shown by default, you have the choice to view all the comments posted on your blog just by clicking this link. You will then be redirected to the Edit Comments page where you can manage and edit the comments.

Figure 2.3 shows how the Recent Comment module appears.

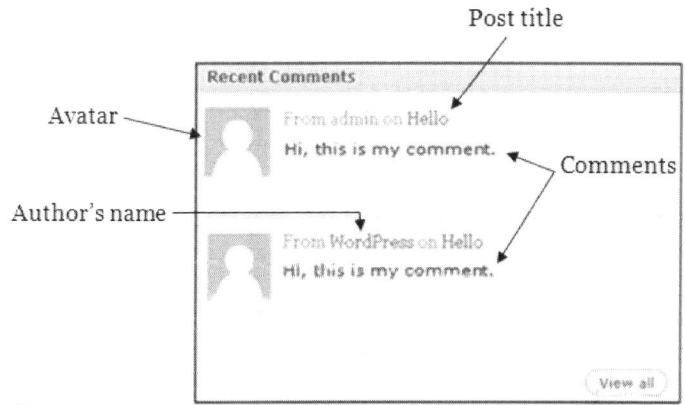

Incoming

Right below the Recent Comments module is the Incoming Links section, as shown in Figure 2.4. Basically, what you will see in this module are the people who created blog posts which link to your blog. Well, of course, if you are a new blogger, there will not be any incoming links listed on this module since people are still not aware of your blog. Do not worry, you will eventually gain readers, and in turn the incoming links.

If you want to edit your Incoming Links module, just follow these steps:
1. Hover your cursor over the title on the Incoming Links section.

2. Click the Configure link.

3. When the Enter the RSS Feed URL Here textbox appears, input the URL of the RSS feed you want to display.

4. Choose the number of items you want to display. The default number is five, and the maximum is 20.

5. Should you want to see the date the link was created, just click the Display Item Date box.

6. Click the Submit button once you are done.

> **Incoming Links**
>
> This dashboard widget queries Google Blog Search so that when another blog links to your site it will show up here. It has found no incoming links... yet. It's okay — there is no rush.

Figure 2.4. The Incoming Links module.

Plugins

This module includes three main titles of WordPress plugins: Most Popular, Newest Plugins, and Recently Updated. However, this module does not let you edit the information shown here.

Plugins module gives you the ability to install, activate, as well as manage the plugins for your blog. In order for you to do so, just follow these steps:

1. Click the Install link right next to the plugin title. There will be a window that will appear, which contains all the information about the plugin.

2. Click the Install Now button if you want to use that plugin.

3. Choose between Activate Plugin (which activates the plugin on your blog) and Return to Plugins Page (which brings you to the Manage Plugins page).

4. Click the Dashboard link which will redirect you back to the dashboard.

Figure 2.5 shows you how the Plugins module appears.

Plugins

Most Popular
SI CAPTCHA Anti-Spam (Install)
Adds CAPTCHA anti-spam methods to WordPress on the comment form, registration form, login, or all. Also is fully WP, WPMU, and BuddyPress compatible.

Newest Plugins
clp.ly (Install)
Plugin for easily adding a "Clip This" button to your WordPress site. For more information, see http://clp.ly/plugins/

Recently Updated
BP Post Buttons (Install)
Adds a button bar to buddypress forum posting textfields

Figure 2.5. The Plugins module.

QuickPress

This module, as shown in Figure 2.6, allows you to easily and quickly create a blog post, hence the term QuickPress. It lets you write a post, and then either save it as a draft or publish it on your blog.

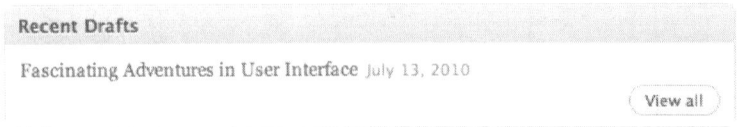

Figure 2.6. The QuickPress module.

Recent Drafts

This section is intended for storing all the blog posts that you have saved as draft. If you are a new blogger, or you just haven't saved any drafts yet, this module will display a "There are no drafts at the moment" message. But later on, as you start creating more and more blog posts, you may eventually save some drafts—which you can just edit and publish later—and these drafts will show up in this module.

Figure 2.7 shows you how the Recent Drafts module appears.

Figure 2.7. The Recent Drafts module.

As you can see, there is only one draft shown since the blogger only has one draft. However, if you have a lot of drafts, only a maximum of five drafts will appear on this module. You can still view all your drafts, of course, just by clicking the View All button, and you will be redirected to the Manage Posts page where you can view, edit, and delete your drafts.

WordPress Blog

Two recent updates from the official WordPress Development Blog (http://wordpress.org/news) will appear on this module (shown in Figure 2.8) by default. The title of the post, the date it was posted, and a short piece from the post will be shown. And when you click the title, you will be brought to the actual post on the WordPress Development Blog.

You can still change which posts this module will display—from WordPress Development Blog to another blog - although it is recommended that you keep the updates from WordPress Development Blog.

Should you decide to change the setting, just do the following steps:

1. Put your mouse over the WordPress Development Blog module title and then click the Configure link.

2. Put in your preferred RSS feed inside the Enter the RSS Feed URL Here text box.

3. Type in your desired title inside the Give the Feed a Title (Optional) text box. As shown, this is optional.

4. Choose a number (the default is 2 and the maximum is 20) from the How Many Items Would You Like to Display drop-down menu.

5. If you want to display the item's content, of the text content from the post, just click the Display Item Content check box. If you do not click this, WordPress will not show you an excerpt from the post; it will only display the title of the post.

6. You can also display the name of the author of the post. Just click the Display Item Author if Available check box.

7. Check the Display Item Date box if you want to see the date the post was made.

8. Once you are done, click the Submit button. Changes will then be applied on your Dashboard page. However, if you think you do not need to apply these changes, just click Cancel.

WordPress Development Blog

WordPress for iPhone/iPad v2.6 Released September 30, 2010
Attention Apple-gadget-owning WordPress users! Have you been using the WordPress iOS app for iPhone and iPad? Or maybe you tried it a while back and thought it wasn't for you? Either way, the new release — v2.6 — will knock your socks off. Why? A bunch of reasons: Video. Record, upload, attach, and play videos [...]

WordPress Trademark Changes Hands September 9, 2010
The WordPress community took a big step forward today when Matt announced that Automattic has donated the WordPress trademark to the non-profit WordPress Foundation. Moving forward, the Foundation will be responsible for safeguarding the trademarked name and logo from misuse toward the end of protecting WordPress and preventing confusion among people trying [...]

Figure 2.8. The WordPress Blog module.

Other WordPress News

This module, as shown in Figure 2.9, is meant for displaying posts from WordPress Planet (http://planet.wordpress.org). By default, the posts that you will see in the section are those that are created by the people involved in the development, design, as well as troubleshooting of WordPress. You will find there some announcements and great information that will help you work around your blog.

Like the other sections, you can also customize the Other WordPress News module. You can change which items you want to appear in this part. You may opt to change them from the official WordPress Planet to other WordPress blogs.

Customizing the Dashboard

Again, WordPress gives you the freedom to change your blogging experience the way you want it to be. You also have the ability to change the appearance of your dashboard.

What makes WordPress one of the best blogging site are the features that it offers to the users. It gives bloggers the freedom to manage as well as customize their pages any way and any time they want. It lets you customize your dashboard so that it will fit all your needs. You can rearrange the modules on your dashboard depending on your own preference, as well as change the links and RSS feed information, and manage other things on your WordPress dashboard to suit your blogging needs. It is your workspace, after all, so you have the freedom to have it the way you want it.

Rearranging the modules

If you think the Right Now module should not be placed where it is placed, or the Incoming links should not be where it is, the good news for you: you can rearrange them. This is definitely the good thing about WordPress: it lets you modify your workspace so that it fits your tastes as well as needs.

If you want to rearrange the order of the modules on your WordPress, just follow these steps:

1. Place your mouse on the title bar of the module that you want to move.

2. Drag the module to your preferred side of the Dashboard. As you drag the module, there will be a light gray box with dotted boarder that will appear on the side of the screen. This box indicates the place where you can place the module.

3. Place the module inside the box. You would notice, too, that the other modules have also changed their positions. For instance, if you placed the Right Now module on the right side of the page, modules on that side will shift down, and then the Recent Comments module will be the one on the top left side of the dashboard.

4. If you want to, you can also close some modules so that they will not appear cluttered on your page. You can click the title bar to collapse, and then click it again to expand the module. Of course, this is optional and is based on your preference.

Just repeat these steps to all the other modules until you are already satisfied with the arrangement of the modules on your page. If you are not satisfied with how it turned out, you can always bring them back by doing the same steps.

Removing modules

While you can rearrange the order of your Dashboard modules, you can also remove unwanted ones. Perhaps, there is a module on your dashboard that you never use. If you want to remove a module, all you have to do is to just click the button that says Screen Options. It is located at the top of your Dashboard. After clicking it, there will be a pop-up menu that will open and it will display the title of the modules that are visible on your dashboard.

There is also a checkbox beside each title, which you can select if you want that particular module to appear on your dashboard, and then deselect if you want to remove that module. Just click those checkboxes that correspond to the modules that you want to appear on your dashboard.

However, should you decide to bring those modules that you have previously removed from your dashboard, just go back to the Screen Options menu and then select the checkboxes for the modules that you want to bring back.

Modifying your Dashboard Layout

There are times when you want to change the layout of your dashboard so that it would be convenient for you to use. Perhaps you want a particular section on your page to be longer than other because it contains more information than the rest. It all depends on your preference, of course, and because we are different people, we all have different preferences when it comes to how we like our space.

Just like in removing modules, you can modify the layout of your dashboard in the Screen Options area. If order for you to work around the layout of your dashboard page, just follow these easy steps:

1. Go to the Screen Options menu by clicking the Screen Options button at the top part of your dashboard page.

2. Select from the Screen Layout Options part the number of columns that you want to be displayed on your dashboard. You can choose from one to four, and the dashboard will automatically adjust afterwards.

3. Just click the Screen Options button once more to go back to the Screen Options Menu and to apply the changes.

Chapter 3: Crafting your Blog Contents

Now that you already know the basics of the WordPress dashboard, you can now proceed to creating your blog contents—which, of course, you will do on the dashboard.

Creating your first post

Your career as a blogger will not get anywhere without starting a single post. Your blog posts are the heart of your blog; without it, you will not be able to start anything.

Creating your blog post is not that hard. In fact, it does not require an expert to compose a post. Just consider typing your blog post as creating an e-mail. You put a title on your post just like how you give your e-mail a subject, and then you write the body, and click the publish button to have your post published and seen by the people all over the world.

The Add New Posts page, as shown in Figure 3.1, is basically your home whenever you have to post a new blog content. This is where you will type in all your blog posts and then either save them as drafts of publish them on your blog.

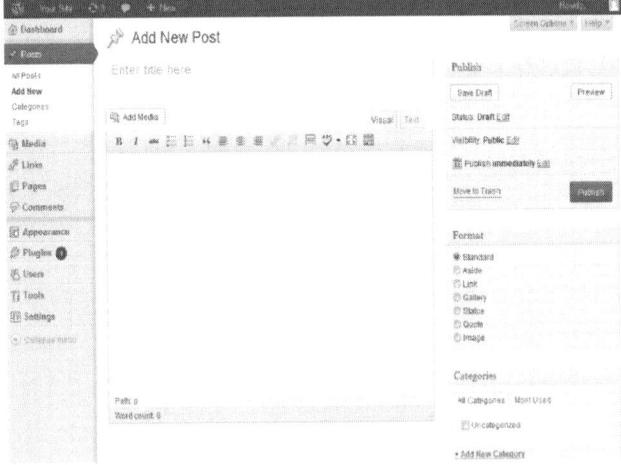

Figure 3.1. The Add New Post page.

You can rearrange the position of all the modules seen on the Add New Posts page. You can also collapse some of these modules so that it won't interfere with the other modules. The only sections that you can't touch and rearrange are the Title box and the Post box; they should remain where they are.

When you create a post, you first have to click the Add New button on the Posts drop down menu. You will be shown the Add New Post page where you will create your post. As you can see, creating a new post is not that complicated. All you have to do is just type the title in the Enter Title Here box. This text box is located at the topmost part of the Add New Post page, as you can see on Figure 3.1. There is no limit as to what title you want to use, of course. This can be anything that you want it to be.

After putting in the post title, you can now write the body of your blog post in the Post box. This box is located just under the Title box. By default, the Post box is set to the Visual Editing mode, where everything can be done in type-and-click method. This means you only have to type in your blog post, and then click a button to spice up your post. For example, if you want to make a part of your post in boldface, you just have to click the B button. Everything is already given to you.

However, you may change the area to the Text Editing mode, wherein all the things that you will do on your text post have to be typed out. For instance, if you want to make a certain part of your text post in boldface, instead of having to click the Bold button, you have to put the HTML tag for this, which is `<strong> </strong>`. Listed below are the basic HTML tags that should come handy when you are in Text Editing mode.

Bold	`<strong> </strong>`
Italic	`<em> </em>`
Underline	`<u> </u>`
Strikethrough	`<strike> </strike>`
Unordered List	`<ul><li> </li></ul>`
Ordered List	`<ol><li> </li></ol>`
Blockquote	`<blockquote> </blockquote>`
Align Left/Center/Right	`<p align="left/center/right"> </p>`
Insert or Edit Link	`<a href="link*"> </a>` *You insert the complete link here
Insert More Tag	`<!—more>`

It is important that you put the end tag `</>` every time you have to end a tag because it indicates the limit in which the tag will apply. For example, if you put the tag `<strong>`, all posts after that tag will be in boldface, unless you put `</strong>` to end the tag.

Posting photos and displaying galleries

An entire page full of text blocks scare readers away because they look dull and exhausting. Therefore, it is important that you give readers some sort of a "resting space" where they can take a break from reading very long texts.

Adding photos to your posts can spice up not just your blog post itself, but your entire blog as well. You make your blog look more interesting by adding images that will help explain contents that you can't put into words. Moreover, images can call the attention of the readers more than blocks of texts can. Generally, images can give your blog posts a more in-depth content. WordPress gives you to ability to upload images within your text posts and as a post itself.

Adding an image to your post

Inserting images to your posts is a very easy task; you can do so with the help of WordPress image uploader. All you have to do is to click the Upload an Image icon on the Add New Post page. After clicking the icon, you will be shown the Add an Image window (as shown in Figure 3.2) that lets you select an image you want to add in your post. The image that you can upload on WordPress can either be from your computer or from the Web.

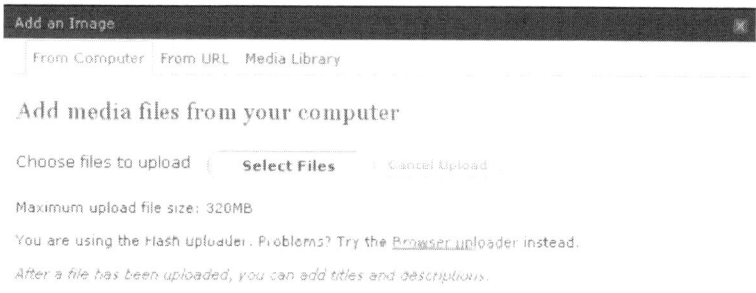

Figure 3.2. The Add an Image window.

Adding an image from your computer is as easy as pie. Just make sure that you are on the From Computer tab where you will see the Select Files button. Once you click that button, select images from your computer's drive and when you have already chosen an image, click the Open button. The maximum file size that you can upload on WordPress is 320 megabytes. Afterwards, you just have to wait for the upload to finish for you to be able to add it on your post. If you do not want to proceed with the upload of the image that you have selected, just click the Cancel Upload button and then repeat the process for another image.

On the other hand, if you want to add an image which you just saw on other web sites or blogs, just click the From URL tab, still on the Add an Image window. There you will see a text box where you are supposed to insert the URL of the image that you want to upload. Make sure that you include the complete URL, with the http:// and, if any, the www portion.

After uploading the image—either from your computer's dive or from the Web—indicate a title for the image in the Image Title box, and then add a description for the image in the Alternate Text box. You may also want to put a caption for the image that you have uploaded, which you will put in the Image Caption text box. You may also opt to include the URL for the image, if you want to link your image to another site. If you do not want to add a link to your image, then your image will not be clickable. You can also set the alignment of your image, whether you want it to be left, center, or right-aligned. You can select the image size as well, wherein you can choose among Thumbnail, Medium, Large, and Full Size images.

Once you are done, you can now click the button that says Insert into Post.

Adding a photo gallery

You may also want to upload more than one photo to your blog, which is known as a photo gallery. WordPress also supports this option, so there is no problem with this.

If you want to add a photo gallery to your blog, just follow these steps:

1. Go to Add an Image window on WordPress and select the images that you want to upload.

2. Click the Save All Changes button (not the Insert into Post button), which is located at the bottom of the window.

3. Click the Gallery tab at the top of the Add an Image window (right next to the From URL tab). Take note that this tab appears only when there are images uploaded.

4. Set the options that you want for your photo gallery. You can set a link for the thumbnails on your gallery, sort your images by menu order, name, or date/time, and either in ascending or descending order, as well as how many columns of images you want to have.

5. Afterwards, save the changes that you have made by clicking the Save All Changes button.

6. To add the gallery in your post, just click the Insert Gallery button.

Audio and Video blogging

WordPress also lets you upload audios and videos on your blog. Just like photographs, these media contents also add flavor to your blog. They appear more interesting to your readers too, and quite easier to use since all they have to do is just hit the play button.

Adding audio files

You can upload any audio files to your blog, depending on what you want the content to be. You may want to send out an audio with you greeting all your readers. Or you may want to share a song cover that you made, or the latest song that you are addicted to. The idea is that audio files can add a personal touch to your blog to some extent.

In order for you to upload an audio file to your blog, just do the following steps:

1. Click the Add Audio icon on the Add New Post page, or on the Edit Post page.

2. Click the Select Files button and then choose the files that you want to upload. Some of the common file extensions that WordPress supports for audio are mp3, wav, midi, and others.

3. Put the title in the Title text box, caption in the Caption text box, and description in the Description text box.

4. You may also want to add a URL for the audio file which will give your post a direct link to the file source.

5. Hit Insert into Post button to add the audio file to your blog post.

Adding video files

Just like audio files, you can also add video files to your blog posts on WordPress. Videos appear to be more interesting to your readers since they can just watch them, instead of let's say read something about them. You can add a video file either from your computer's drive or from the Web.

To add a video file from your computer, just follow these steps (and make sure that you are on the From Computer tab):

1. Click the Add Video icon on the Add New Post page, or on the Edit Post page.

2. Click the Select Files button and then choose the video file that you want to upload.

3. Put the title in the Title text box, caption in the Caption text box, and description in the Description text box for your video post.

4. You may also want to add a URL for the video file which will give your post a direct link to the file source.

5. Hit Insert into Post button to add the video file to your blog post.

On the other hand, you can also add a video on your blog which you can get from other websites. You just have to go to the From URL tab on the Add Video window. Then follow these steps:

1. Type in the complete URL or the internet address of the video that you want to use in the URL text box. Make sure that you include the http:// and the www.

2. Put a title for your video in the Title text box, but this is optional.

3. If you are already done, just click the Insert into Post button.

You can also embed a video from other websites on your blog. For example, if you want to insert a video from YouTube and you want your readers to view that video the YouTube-way, you have to embed that video. In order to do so, just put the video's URL in your post and WordPress will automatically detect it. But you have to make sure that the Auto-Embed feature on your blog's Media Settings is enabled. You can also enter the size of your video and indicate the size and the width of your video.

Some of the websites that WordPress embeds to your blog automatically include YouTube, Vimeo, DailyMotion, Flickr, Viddler, PhotoBucket, and others.

Chapter 4: The WordPress Community

In blogging, it is also important that you are a part of a much bigger community. It is a lot helpful if you are connected to other people who will in turn read and support your blog as well as give your help whenever you need them.

Finding other users

Your blogging experience will not be complete if you do not connect with other WordPress users. There are millions of users on WordPress that you will not run out of connection. As a matter of fact, there will be more or less 200 million results when you Google WordPress.

It is undeniable that a lot of people are already on WordPress, which means that you can be connected to as many as you want to. But more than that, there are also some Web sites that also feature WordPress-related things, which can help you get connected with other WordPress users.

  a. *WP Tavern* (http://wptavern.com). This site gives you the latest news as well as discussions that are related to WordPress. More so, it also lets the visitors interact with other users and talk about anything about WordPress.

  b. *WP Candy* (http://wpcandy.com). This website covers anything WordPress-related, from news to tutorials to important tools. It also features some people that are popular on WordPress.

  c. *WordCast*(http://wordcastnet.com). This website offers weekly Internet radio show, or *podcast*, which also talks about topics that are related to WordPress as well as blogging and social media in general.

Finding professionals

Aside from other users, you can also look for WordPress professionals that can help you as a blogger as well as make your blogging experience a whole lot easier.

a. *WordPress designers.* As the name itself suggests, these people are the ones who are well-knowledgeable about designing WordPress pages. They know how to work around graphic designing and even CSS (Cascading Style Sheet). They are usually the ones who have the ability to create themes for WordPress accounts and make your blog look more appealing to your readers than ever.

b. *WordPress developers.* These people are the ones who are in-charge of maintaining and developing the WordPress site. They understand the WordPress motto "Code is poetry" more than anybody does. They are the ones who are responsible for storing databases and other contents and data of your blogs.

c. *WordPress Consultants.* These people may not be friends with codes unlike the first two groups of WordPress professionals, but they can help you get in touch with the latter. They serve as consultants who help you configure what you have to do with your blog and how you can make your blogging experience better.

Contributing to WordPress

You can also serve as a contributor to WordPress, especially if you have skills in some areas that are related to blogging. Here are some ways on how you can contribute to WordPress:

a. *Providing codes.* If you know how to work around codes, then WordPress totally needs you. You can be a part of WordPress developers by contributing codes to them. Just submit your codes through the WordPress Trac (http://dore.trac.wordpress.org).

b. *Testing.* You can also contribute to WordPress by testing WordPress beta version as well as reports your own experience on WordPress, especially if you encounter bugs and other problems. The developers will in turn monitor these and work on the troubleshooting.

c. *Documenting.* There is the WordPress Codex that stores all the documentations for WordPress. You can contribute by sending your own documentation to WordPress through http://codex.wordpress.org.

d. *Giving Tutorials.* You can also be a contributor by providing some tutorials that can help other bloggers. All you have to do is just create a blog post containing tutorials and publish it for others to see.

e. *Joining the Support Forums.* You can also join the WordPress Support Forums where you can share your talents and knowledge to other WordPress users.

f. *Volunteering for the WordPress events.* You can also help in the presentations for the WordPress events, which include MeetUps and WordCamps.

Joining events on WordPress

As mentioned in the previous section, there are two types of WordPress events, which are MeetUps and WordCamps. Joining these live events will surely make your blogging experience better than ever.

   a. *WordPress MeetUps.* Usually, WordPress users organize monthly MeetUps where they can meet each other within their area. In those meetups, there are organizers, speakers, and attendees that join the event. You can look for MeetUps near you by going to the MeetUp Web site (http://meetup.com).

   b. *WordPress WordCamps.* While MeetUps happen every month, WordCamps happen every year. This event is way larger than the MeetUp and there are more participants. Usually, people all around the country join this annual event along with other personalities, and major cities in the United States and other countries host this event. You can look for the upcoming WordCamp near your place by going to WordCamp's website (http://wordcamp.org).

If there are no MeetUps and WordCamps near you, then perhaps it is about time that you start and organize one! You can know more about organizing WordPress live events at http://wordcamps.org.

Conclusion

Thank you again for downloading this book!

I hope this book was able to help you learn the ways on how you would be able to start blogging using WordPress. I also hope that this book was able to provide clear step-by-step guides on how you would be able to start blogging on WordPress as well as how you would be able to expand your connection with other people.

Finally, if you enjoyed this book, please take the time to share your thoughts and post a review on Amazon. It'd be greatly appreciated!

Thank you and good luck!

Check Out My Other Books

Below you'll find some of my other popular books that are popular on Amazon and Kindle as well. Simply click on the links below to check them out. Alternatively, you can visit my author page on Amazon to see other work done by me.

If the links do not work, for whatever reason, you can simply search for these titles on the Amazon website to find them.

Printed in Great Britain
by Amazon.co.uk, Ltd.,
Marston Gate.